Contents

What are flowers?

Flowers are parts of flowering plants that produce **seeds**. The seeds will grow into new plants. So a flower has an important job in the life cycle of a plant.

▼ People buy beautiful, sweet-smelling flowers to decorate their homes.

See how plants grow

Flowers

Nicola Edwards

WAYLAND

Copyright © Wayland 2006

Published in Great Britain in 2006 by Wayland,
a division of Hachette Children's Books

This paperback edition published in 2008 by
Wayland.

Editor: Penny Worms
Senior Design Manager: Rosamund Saunders
Designer: Elaine Wilkinson

Wayland,
338 Euston Road
London NW1 3BH

British Library Cataloguing in Publication Data
Edwards, Nicola
        Flowers. - (See how they grow)
        1. Flowers - Juvenile literature
        I. Title
        582.1'3

ISBN 9780750255882

Printed in China

Wayland is a division of Hachette Children's
Books, an Hachette Livre UK company.

www.hachettechildrens.co.uk

The publishers would like to thank the following
for allowing us to reproduce their pictures in
this book:
Corbis images: cover & 7 (George H. H. Huey),
8 (Irwan), 11 (Herbert Kehrer), 14 (Reuters),
18 (Hamish Park). Ecoscene: 12 (Vicki Coombs),
16 (Michael Gore). Getty images: title page &
23 (Dan Bigelow), 4 (Richard I'Anson), 6 (Gay
Bumgarner), 9 (Jack Dykinga), 10 (Steve
Satushek), 15 (Steve Hopkin), 17 (Rebecca
Emery), 20 (Harald Sund), 21 (Nicolas DeVore).
Photolibrary: 13 (Vaughn Greg). Wayland Picture
Library: 5, 19, 22.

Flowers come in a huge variety of shapes, sizes and colours. They are most common in spring and summer. Some flowers have a strong **scent**, others no scent at all.

▶ These flowers are cherry blossom from a cherry tree.

Flower Fact

Many trees produce flowers. So do some vegetable plants, such as courgettes.

Where do flowers grow?

Walk around your local area and you'll see flowers in many different places. People plant flowers in their gardens, window boxes and hanging baskets. There are often colourful displays of flowers in parks.

▼ A meadow in summer is full of wild flowers.

Look out for flowers growing wild in fields, woods and by the roadside, or pushing their way up through gaps in the pavement.

▼ Sunflowers are grown on farms for their seeds and oil.

Flower Fact

Cereals that we eat such as rice and wheat are flowering plants.

Flowers around the world

Flowers grow in most parts of the world except near the North and South Poles where it is too cold. Plants such as orchids live in hot, wet **tropical rainforests**. Orchid flowers are colourful and some grow in shapes that make them look like insects.

▼ The massive rafflesia flower grows in Malaysia's rainforests.

Mountain flowers grow in clumps close to the ground. This stops them from being damaged by strong winds.

▼ Flowers can even grow in dry deserts. These cacti are flowering plants.

9

How do flowers grow?

Some flowering plants start life as a **bulb**. Others begin as seeds. They all need soil and water to start growing. As the seed or bulb grows, a green shoot or **stem** pushes upwards through the soil towards the light. The plant needs water, light and air to grow bigger.

▶ A plant's **roots** take in the water and **nutrients** it needs to grow.

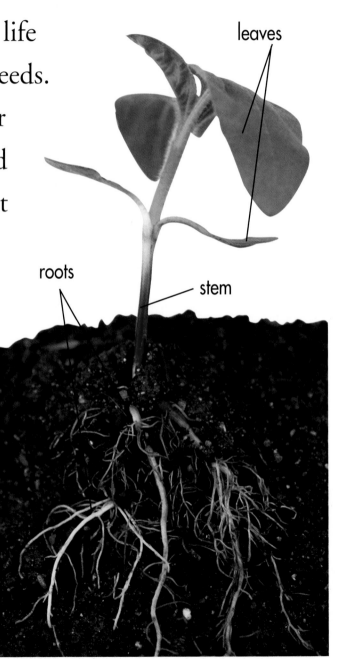

leaves

roots

stem

flower bud

Buds form on branches. Inside the buds, flowers and leaves are growing.

leaf bud

11

Parts of a flower

Petals give flowers their beautiful colours. The petals surround the inner parts of the flower which are needed to make seeds. Some of the inner parts of a flower are male and others are female. The male parts of a flower produce **pollen**.

carpel
female part of the flower

stamen
male part of the flower

pollen

▶ Look inside this lily at all the different parts.

▼ Pollen is like dust. It sticks to the flower but comes off easily.

Colours and smells

Flowers have colourful petals and strong scents to attract insects such as butterflies and bees. Flowers provide insects with food in the form of pollen and a sugary liquid called **nectar**.

When they feed, the insects move pollen from the male parts of a flower to the female parts. This is called **pollination**.

Flower Fact

The patterns on flowers show insects where to find nectar and pollen.

▼ Some insects are attracted by the rotting meat smell of the titan arum.

▼ As this bee brushes against the flower it is dusted with yellow pollen.

What happens after pollination?

With some flowering plants, such as grasses, the wind carries the pollen. After pollination a grain of pollen joins with the female part of the flower and a seed begins to grow. This is called **fertilization**.

▼ Some flowers are pollinated by animals and birds, such as this hummingbird.

Flower Fact

Wind-pollinated flowers are less colourful and don't have a strong scent.

▼ Different coloured flowers grow when one plant is pollinated by another.

17

Flowers and fruits

Once a seed has begun to grow, a flower's work is over. Its petals wither and fall off. A **fruit** forms around the seeds. Some fruits such as tomatoes and papayas have lots of seeds, while others such as apples and pea pods have fewer.

▶ When each strawberry flower dies, a fruit begins to grow. Can you see the seeds?

Flower Fact

Plants such as ferns and mosses do not make flowers.

Other fruits such as peaches, cherries and mangoes contain just one seed.

▲ After a dandelion has flowered, seeds are left behind. They are then carried away by the wind.

How do we use flowers?

Flowering plants provide us with food such as fruit, vegetables and cereals, and we also use them to make materials such as cotton and linen for clothes. Oils from flowers are used in medicines and perfumes.

▼ Flowers brighten our gardens and parks with their colours and scents.

We use flowers to decorate our homes and places of worship. People carry or wear flowers on special days such as weddings and festivals.

▼ People from the Cook Islands welcome visitors with flowers.

Grow your own flowers

See how a flower grows for yourself.
Fill a flower pot with soil. Plant a bulb by
pushing it gently into the soil until it is
well covered. Put the pot on a windowsill.

bulb

water

soil

◀ Here's what
you need to grow
a flower indoors.

pot

Flower Fact

When seeds or bulbs
start to grow, this is
called **germination**.

Water the soil and keep it moist. Record what happens. When does the first green shoot appear? When do the buds start to form on the stem? When does the first flower open?

▼ You can also plant seeds and bulbs in the garden.

Glossary

bud
The parts of a flowering plant in which leaves and flowers form.

bulb
Some flowering plants start their life as a bulb. Bulbs store food for the developing plant.

fertilization
When the male and female parts of a plant merge.

fruit
The part of a flowering plant that contains its seeds.

germination
The process by which seeds start to grow into plants.

nectar
A sweet liquid produced by flowers to attract insects.

nutrients
Food that is sucked up by the roots of a plant from the soil.

petals
The colourful, often scented parts of a flower that protect its inner parts.

pollen
A yellow or orange dust that a female part of a flower needs to receive to form a seed.

pollination
The process by which pollen is transferred from the male to the female parts of a flower.

root
The parts of a plant that hold it in the soil and take in water and nutrients.

scent
A nice smell.

seed
Many flowering plants start life as a seed.

stem
The part of a flowering plant that holds it upright.

tropical rainforests
Forests that grow in areas where it is hot and wet.

Index